# Thirsty Dreams

101 Songs and Poems about Doing Your Own
Thing, Including Being Independent, Embarking,
Sharing, Falling, Maintaining, Moving On,
Hats and Perspectives

Books by Matt Kavan

*Flopping on the Deck*
*The Forest That Knows*
*Thirsty Dreams*
*Here For a Moment*
*Here's To*
*The Morning Catch*

# Thirsty Dreams

101 Songs and Poems about Doing Your Own
Thing, Including Being Independent, Embarking,
Sharing, Falling, Maintaining, Moving On,
Hats and Perspectives

**Matt Kavan**

Matt Kavan
2014

First Printing: 2014

ISBN: 978-1-312-36879-8

Matt Kavan
www.mattkavan.com

Book Cover Graphics: The painting Horizons was created by Paul Kavan.

Ordering Information:
Special discounts are available on quantity purchases by corporations, associations, educators, and others. For details, contact the publisher at the above listed address.

# Dedication

To George and Ed.

# Contents

# Introduction

Getting started and doing something on your own can be both an extremely simple and difficult thing to do. It's simple when starting, as you're just building or planning your idea and haven't received too much feedback, and gets more difficult the farther or longer you go. As most of the time when starting something new will end in failure, starting a business or freelancing is no different. Then again, people love to play games, with the more variables the better, but as soon as a game is mastered, can win without issue, it becomes boring, repetitive, no fun, and most likely onto something else.

While there are many different games, the ones with the most variables are the ones where you're the most involved, are juggling many different activities, but where you're still generally in control of your own actions and the appropriate outcome. When failing, it's simply another lesson learned and most likely when trying again will sail right past it, straight into the next wall and the story is repeated. By the time you have anything figured out, and others are recognizing it, you probably don't realize it, don't believe it's real, or have a lingering suspicion that something bad will happen, the wall will reappear and if you don't keep your eyes open, will smash into it yet again.

Of course, there are occasional successes, accomplishments and celebrations, but usually when looking back, the best laughs are from the truly massive screw-ups or experiences, telling yourself "what was I thinking?" and laughing, but that's the way it goes. Somebody from a nature perspective could say that's the curse of evolving, realizing that everything you've done in the past or doing in the present is wrong, but at the same time, you need to do those things to get to wherever you'll be. And sure, you could hang out on the same step for awhile or intentionally forever, but whether we like it or not things change, something happens to the step, it gets overcrowded, and to reach the same idea of what it was like when you got there, you have to change.

Thirsty Dreams is a collection of songs and poems about doing your own thing, including some overall perspectives of trying to be independent, embarking or getting started on something new, sharing it with others or trying to sell it, hitting walls and falling, keeping steady and maintaining your direction, occasionally moving on, as well as the hats and perspectives you get along the way.

# Being Independent

## At Your Command

In the mountains of yore
Flows a stream from the core
Traveling down the nooks and bends
To the shore where the cycle ends
Whatever happens along the way
Are the lessons that we take
Sink or swim or a little of both
Staying shallow or out of depth
In the end it's never what's planned
Says the unknown fate at your command

## Being Defined

Some people say
They know the way
Being defined
Mostly astray

## Currencies

All types of different currencies
Trading and exchange
For work, products and services
Common and the strange
Cash for pay as you go
Credit with interest to treble
Barter with skills you know
Dying or living struggle
Which is better, which is worse
Changing by the day
Until your own a tragic curse
The value drifts away
Down the stream with the seasons
A deluge or the spring
The snowman tries to argue reason
A bird discovers wings
A tree finds its roots
A turtle seeks the sea
A niche for making boots
Walking roads with glee

**Embracing the Fool**


Some people feel a need to escape
From all of the tragedies of another day
Where can they go, what can they do
Embracing the part of a fool on the loose

Some say they're crazy, follow no rules
Or a bit lazy, pay attention to clues
Seeing the signs, from forgotten lore
Hearing the songs, brighten the core

Sometimes it works out, mostly not so much
Have to move on, or left with a crutch
I admit a bit sad, the past that was had
What can you do, a world spinning fast

Try to slow it down, good luck with that
Nature in command, a primitive cast
So much more, than dragons and snakes
Once you've been alive, perspectives to play

## Hearing the Song

There's so many times, that we're all alone
Don't know where we're going, no sense of home
Bouncing along, the merry go round of life
Hearing the song, to carry through the strife

Heard many times before, but can't ignore
The tunes that play, open new doors
Going high and low, connecting with a dream
Of where we're from, a forgotten stream

Going higher and higher, never to fall
As long as it plays, banging the gong
A chorus of strings, up and down the scales
With bells to ring, a never ending trail

Through rocks and trees, it'll never stop
Some people pick up, where others left off
Passing on the baton, for another song
Where it ends, where we belong

Into the dawn, the music plays
Nobody declares, a brand new day
Where will you go, what you will do
Ends with the clown, joker or fool

**Home of the Sphere**


Looking for a path, searching for a road
Taking me where meant to be, some might call it a home
Scanning the horizons, climb the highest peak
Following scenes from a dream, a game of hide and seek

With nowhere left to go, and nothing left to do
I make a stand where I am, some say a fool
Building up foundations, one block at a time
Making steps for a higher trek, not a tower for the blind

Years going by, a ball fell from the sky
About ten feet high and wide, where it's from, how and why
Touch a spot, a perspective cube met
Light it up, fill the cup, see the surface of a life set

Going deeper, past the top layer
Shapes and sounds to surround, abstract to bare
How deep does it go, scaling with the flow
The sphere getting clearer, in the middle is home

**In the New**


We're all alone in this great big world
Yes it's true there have been friends
Family too but when it's through
Depends on the boat you're in
From a lake, a river and ocean
It changes all the time
Flying too at high noon
No words to describe

Chorus
Here's to all the struggles, we've made it through
Here's to all the jokes, escaping blue
In the new

Things might go well, it seems all fine
But as any gambler knows
Play long enough, with the same old hand
The odds will surely show
Able to see, planting a tree
In wastelands, desert dunes
When the deluge arrives, hop on a boat to ride
Hear the calling of the loon

Chorus

When you finally get to the boat of boats
Look around the scene
All the rowers, faces you know
As if, from a dream
Where we're all headed, a different place
Sometimes you row or bail
Where it is, gone from the cave
Let the wind, blow the sail

Chorus

**Learning to Stand**

Chop down the tree
As fast as you can
Growing your own
Learning to stand


**Lost Lands**

The highlands and lowlands
Scattered across the earth
Living in the lost land
Knowing what it's worth

## Of Each and Every Dream

I'll have my coffee, sometime after dark
A drink in the morning, happy hour starts
Drive cross the country, without any sleep
Fish in the rain, no shallow all deep
Some say slow down, smell the flowers
Around me, nature screams
What can I say when climbing the towers
Of each and every dream

I'll cross some lines, to see if they're real
Tell a few jokes, show how I feel
I'll pay all my dues, then burn up the lists
Seek out the fool, without any tricks
Mostly a stranger, with nothing to lose
Adapting to, the new scene
If down anyway, I'll laugh with the loons
Of each and every dream

I'll disappear, without leaving a trace
May reappear, with a different face
Had dozens of jobs, all kinds of perspectives
Maybe too far, a detour directive
Some say I should settle on just one thing
Just like, a machine
Hard to do with so many bells to ring
Of each and every dream

**Pulling Strings**

In a world full of puppets
Who pulls the strings
Is it the ones with the money
With interest on things
The ones with the guns
With offers of orders
The ones getting votes
Popularity taking over
The ones that dream
Maps of the future
The ones that scream
Wanting forever
All of these ones
And so many more
But the one inside you
Cannot be ignored

## See the Bird That Flew

It's getting past noon, how much longer to last
Before the sun sets and my fate is cast
Such a mystery when looking to be
Never quite knowing if ending in the sea

Hear the sirens singing a hypnotic tune
Drawing you in, by the light of the moon
Jump off a ledge, trying to fly
Too far from the hedge, hear the guardians sigh

See the wasteland no fear to command
Nobody is watching where you stand
Walking tall and strong, banging the gong
Playing the flute and singing the song

Chorus
You have to wonder why it took so long
Tried everything, ended up wrong and blue
Only at the end, nobody a friend
The anchors are cast, see the bird that flew

Hop on board the boat from the sky
To the shining stars for the infinite ride
We'll meet again, at the distant place
Until then, gone without a trace

Chorus

## The Stranger

Seeing the stranger
On the long open road
Sometimes he finds a manger
A temporary home
Mostly he keeps walking
In the sun he's alone

Chorus
Aren't we all, just like the stranger
When we fall and amend
From the land, growing stronger
Getting higher in the wind

Others try to join
Getting burned from the heat
Some will charge a coin
Thankful he has feet
Mostly a distraction
All the groups that he meets

Chorus

Many years later
Who knows where you'll find
The stranger that keeps walking
Reading all the signs
If you ever want to see again
A long, upward climb

Chorus

Heading to the mountains
To the highest peak
Drinking from a fountain
Honey turns to mead
Building up a fire
In the smoke you'll see

Chorus

## We're All a Little Bit Odd


Sometimes when we feel, just a little bit strange
For speaking our own mind
Getting the look, you've become a new stray
You're of a different kind

Chorus
Yeah, well, we're all just a little bit odd
Yes it's true, we're not even
We're all a little bit odd
The one, three, five, seven, nine, eleven
We're all a little bit odd
We know nothing is for certain
We're all a little bit odd
Or not a little, but a lot

Find independence, chart a new path
Stretching out and complete
Walk through the woods, make it to last
Rising to a higher peace

Chorus

So much more, than tugging the core
The matter that you're in
The downward spirals, the box of lore
All the way until the end

Chorus

**With No Debt**

With no debt
Nobody owns thee
Call it a curse
Born too free
Every fall
Is from your own
Getting up
The tree has grown


**Xerox Expense**

Copy an idea, not your own expense
Losing the value, how to do again
The process, the system or equation
Variables needed to be able
To see the next steps from failures before
Sprinting too far and viewing a world
After the ones that you're finishing up
Seeds are planted, empty the cup
Leaving to flow, others get drunk
The quench never slows, stakes have been sunk
Milking the cow, charging a toll
Too many hands, where does it go
Many years later, the tree has been grown
Past all the steps from stories of lore
How can it be copied, how can it be known
Chopped down for paper, a Xerox is told
Why or how, to what end or purpose
Lost in the nuts, the squirrels have taken

# Embarking

**A Chance to Begin**

Hearing the crackles
Of a new found idea
Add some more kindling
Losing the fear

Gather some logs
Make it go higher
Start up the dance
With music or choir

Around in a circle
With smoke to rise
Up from the middle
Carry no lies

To the stars above
Or elsewhere no matter
Letting it out
Growing much faster

For the remains
Ashes in the wind
Giving the idea
A chance to begin

## Foundations to Stand

Gather all your energy
As much as you can
Build it up, make it grow
Foundations to stand


## Gathering and Storing

It's not to believe
That creates the dream
Gathering and storing
The Ka to be


## Go, Go, Go

Go, go, go, with all that you can
No mind for others, they'll think that you're mad
Write a book, play a tune, start a new biz
Make up a recipe, home brew it is
And after that, well, you know where it goes
A never ending staircase, planting to grow
With twists and turns for all of your falls
Only much later can you see where you are

**Into Which We're Thrown**

Gather it up, into a ball
See the brightened glow
It doesn't matter how small
A spark will start the flow
The waves will roll, hear the sound
Ride it if you can
In the wind, learn to spin
Never touch the land
To the end, hard to tell
Which way it will go
Nobody knows the unknown plan
Into which we're thrown


**Letting it Through**

Why do I do it
To conquer the fear
Letting it through
And all is clear


**Making**

The bread of life
Trees of creation
In the end
From our making

**Meant to Know**

The world is what you make it
From which the waters flow
Follow dreams to take you
Through horizons meant to know


**Missing Pieces**

I have a new idea, damn the torpedoes
Nothing to lose, loosen the arrows
Maybe it'll work, maybe it won't
Never find out, until it's been grown
Will it bare fruit, sour or sweet
Barrels of loot, shoes for the feet
Taking much longer, need to be stronger
Leaving the anger, surviving the winter
Until the next spring, finding out what you got
Growing up green, returning from lost
The dreams that were started, so long ago
Have finally found, their place in the show


**Name to Claim**

Let's get the show started
Enough with the games
The course has been charted
Only the name to claim

**Nothing to Lose**

I'll put in my time
I'll pay all my dues
If not going fine
Nothing to lose


**Quixote Directive**

Seeking the battle, climbing the stone
Testing your mettle, travel some roads
In the end, lose or win
Are merely glimpses, of what can begin


**Strategies and Plans**

Make up all your plans
Strategies at your will
Castles made of sand
Washing waves, left is nill

**The Abyss**

When looking for something
And everywhere you have gone
Into the abyss
Where answers do belong

Sometimes far away
Mostly around the corner
You know you're almost there
When you become a foreigner

Stay too long and miss it
No turning back the time
Back to the abyss
Where the dreams begin to rise

**The Source**

Dreams are the
Ultimate source of energy
Sparking the inertia
Imagine infinity

**Use Em or Lose Em**

The days only last so long
Use em or lose em
Add a verse to the song
Fill up the vacuum

**Vacuums**

Open holes, nature abhors
So its said, fruit galore
Troughs to find, wants to meet
Needs and signs, a welcome greet

Leaders lost, replaced with strings
Disconnected, until grounded is
Either way, a temporary stay
So many holes, open every day

From what you see or in your head
When awake or dreams in bed
Maybe small but if left alone
Growing over the entire world

Fixing whatever's working
Pull the bottom card and sinking
Best to build, climb new steps
Leave the rest, holes to stop

Are vacuums good or bad
Cleaning up or chaos had
Suck you down in the bottomless pit
Until the rise with solid fits

**Violet**

Hot and cold, see the steam rising
Back and forth, perpetual motion
Night and day, extremes of a scene
Red and blue, a balance to see
Try to go further, lost in the view
The unknown edge, glimpses of new

# Sharing

**Answers to Critics**

Hey no problem
It happens all the time
In the past would be a lynching
Speaking from your mind

Just the way it goes
Nobody is perfect
Still doing pretty good
If one in ten don't like it

Maybe you know better
I'm been wrong before
Walking versus talking
Answers versus lore

**Choices to Fate**

I create what I sell
In the currency of the day
If all going well
Choices to fate

**Chop Down the Tree**

Chop down the tree
Burn up the stump
Dig up the roots
Until all is undone

Pay no attention
To others that disapprove
They do not understand
What you're trying to prove

Make an example
To show how it's done
How to go further
Burn in the sun

Maybe they'll get it
Maybe they'll see
Who really cares
When flowing to sea


**Denial**

Being denied
Find the truth inside
Go with the flow
For more to know

**Find the Magic Ride**

Throw me all your punches
Cut me with all your knives
It's just what I needed
To find the magic ride


**How Can I Make a Buck**

How can I make a buck
Without feeling like selling out
It doesn't matter when out of luck
No point to cry or shout
So what to when feeling stuck
Back it up and load the truck
Nobody knows until the dice are thrown
How can I make a buck

**Left Has Gone to Wasteland**


What's good, what's bad
Decided by others
To protect or direct
Fluffing some feathers

In the end is a trend
Every lesson that's learned
The only way at your expense
Travel through the burn

While I appreciate
Your rules and critiques
Can't you see, I'm drowning
All the chains that you make

So when you see, I'm doing my thing
Don't try to correct me
Unless you can, extend the song
Springboards from reflecting

That's it, no left more to say
I hope you understand
I'm sure I'm wrong, but it's where I belong
Left has gone to wasteland

**Let It Loose**

Get it out, let it loose
Open the cage, free the noose
Accepted or not, I don't really care
Into the new, after it's shared


**Paying Dues**

Feeling nervous to share what you've created
So much could go wrong, butterflies are active
Have to deal with the critics that cackle
Or hearing the crickets from foreign travels
It's no matter, millions have done before
When looking back, a laugh not ignored
For taking a chance, leaving your mark
Able to move on, after it's done
Which is another purpose of sharing
Letting it out, more room for the making
Good or bad, what can you expect
Sharing the new, awaken the dead
For them or you, both can be had
Escaping the blue, laughing from sad
For we've all been there, a tired old shoe
Playing for fare, paying a due

**Send in the Clowns**

Freeing the baggage
Letting it go
Send in the clowns
Start up the show


**Spinning Wheels**

Getting defensive, of light shining on
All of my struggles, ending up wrong
Trying everything, get told it's not enough
Do it all again, pouring out the cup

Crash and burn never learn how to stand up straight
On my knees begging please, forgive past mistakes
Arriving late for the fate, have another beer
Drown it out see the now, eliminate the fear

Nothing happens no control, time to roll
Keep on spinning never winning, pay another toll
Start again meet a friend, at least for a while
Never lasting long, not every song, ends with a smile

Try again a later send, you end up alone
The way it goes, in the ocean flowing to a home
See the salmon no denying, swimming against the current
Could be you, play a fool, each and every moment

**Where All Are In the Band**


Sharing with others, not always so gloomy
Sometimes an encore, you'll be receiving
Hands waving wildly, shouting for more
Until nothing left, fall on the floor

Or others will say, you should turn pro
Helping for booking, a sold out show
Maybe they're right, creeps in your head
Making up plans, full speed ahead

Approaching the cliff, too late to slow down
Falling again, when nobody has shown
How did it happen, what was the difference
A random crossing, maybe the audience

So what do you do, with so many mixed signals
Listen to all, a puppet to jingle
Or keep on going, with your own direction
No more regrets, upon reflection

If they like it great, building some springboards
If not oh well, locked up the doors
That only leave you walking, a bit faster on return
No bother for the knocking, lessons have been learned

Until sooner or later, will find a welcome scene
Where all is new and nobody sees the dream
Adapting and playing, sharing with your friends
Riding in the boat that floats, where all are in the band

# Falling

**Another Pass**

On a trip or adventure
Problems you may have
Nothing you can do
But find another pass


**Backups**

Having a backup
Will surely be used
Anything to escape
Accepting the new


**Burn to Learn**

Connecting to worlds
Both high and below
Every step, burn to learn
Growing right to know

## Change

How can you ever change
Step out of the box
Seeing the world
Connecting the dots
Plotting a line
Up, down or sideways
Calling left and right
Road stops or highways
Dropping out of a scene
Planting in another
Waiting for the rain
And sun to discover
What it ends up growing
Maybe short or tall
All from your tending
After every fall


## Failing

To fail is to learn
The curse of evolving
Success is a menace
Slowing to stalling

To fail is to burn
And rise from the ashes
So says the phoenix
Playing with matches

To fail is to earn
From your expense
Only to return
Joking with an audience

**Losing the Dream**

As the fire slowly burns
The fiddler watches turns
Shows to entertain the mind
From realities not inclined
The days to months to years
Adding up as the end is near
The bottles stacking miles high
No longer any question of why
Too late to start over again
Or a boat to find a friend
Just the way it goes, before you know
Losing the dream starts the slow


**Out of the Shell**

Why do you do it
Looking for pain
More than your fill
Drive you insane
Either or
Pacing the cell
Feeling alive
Out of the shell

**Repetition is Past**

Whoops, too far, shouldn't have taken that last step
Never knowing until walking, when the water freezes up
Or out for a stroll, on a dark and stormy night
Going with the flow, until the waterfall sight
How far you will fall, never knowing until landing
Could be just a bit or a staircase never ending
Collecting again, resting for awhile
How far you fell, showing a smile
For the next time you'll know, when to start moving different
Maybe fast or slow, depending on the current
Soon enough you'll be past it, enjoy it while it lasts
Never lasting long, when repetition is past


**Tired**

Feeling so comfy
In bed with a pillow
Then again so tired
Could be nails from a steeple

**Trying**

It's better to have tried and lose
Than never having tried at all
Or it's said there is no try
Do or not, no fall
Which is better it all depends
On the hats that you wear
Choices found or only one
The road that's right to bare


**Weary**

Work until you fall
Over in a heap
Feel your eyes closing
Fading off to sleep

# Maintaining

## Alive Until Tomorrow

We wake in the morning
Or in the afternoon
Sometimes in the evening
Start at midnight too

Stepping in the world
Or in a type of scene
Clocks setting down the rules
A battle against the dreams

That started as a child
Or on a late night bend
Keep alive until tomorrow
Or twist and spin in the wind

## An Ending

Keep me in the shade
Keep me in the shadows
You can't stop the rain
Or the clouds that gather
Sooner or later
A drizzle to a deluge
No need for a trader
To barter a refuge
When all is said and done
A grade to a level
Stand in the sun
A spade or a shovel

## Brew Another Pot of Coffee

Brew another pot of coffee, the day isn't yet done
Watching the setting and rising, of the cycling sun
Too much to do, all the hurdles to clear
Bridges to cross, losing time and fear
Just another few steps further, before the big crash
After that a few more, no time for looking back
Days, weeks and months go by, a steady upward climb
With of course the detour ride, when blinded from the signs
Where it goes we'll never know, the mystery of the journey
On a paved or gravel road, always is the yearning
Of a place to settle down and start up once again
Brew another pot of coffee, seems to be the trend

**Chilled Dreams**


Sometimes when you can barely crawl
Maybe sick or after a fall
All distractions are gone with the breeze
As you settle down, feel the freeze
Chills everywhere from a fading core
Need a spark to grow for more
Fuel the fire and let it run
Hear the silence before the gun
Or not this time, maybe sleep is fine
Perhaps some dreams of a steeper climb
Or so you thought as you close your eyes
Before you awake you're given lies
Of a time from so long ago
When all was well and still had hope
Carrying along as if nothing happened
Between then and now the trappings
That you thought you escaped but never did
All you found were spots that hid
That seemed to work out all fine indeed
Except for the remnants of lingering dreams
Will they ever go away sometimes you ponder
What do they mean to stick around longer
Maybe a test when not ready to see
Still holding onto the fallen leaves
Never the same a repetitive drunk
Those are the ones I wake up sunk
Others are more inspiring I suppose
Finding the new and see where it goes
Wondering if real or a forgotten past
To settle a score or extend the track
So many places and people I've met
Swimming in my brain and stuck in my head
Sometimes you control the way it goes
Others you sit and go with the flow
After thirty days I'll be a bit stronger
Trying to harness the dreams to remember


Direct their flow to a different road

Waking up my feet will know
Will they follow or more of the same
Chilled from dreams, a heading is claimed

**Ending Up Blue**


Feeling the fog, rolling on in
The wind blows the hair, across your face
With a drizzle falling, the chill becoming
You're all alone in the modern rat race
It's getting high noon, not that you can see
The sun has left, clouds are roaming free
All bundled up, having a beer
Up goes the glass, raising a cheer

Your hands going numb, hard to write any more
But you feel the need, have to go forward
So much to learn, writing to earn
A piece of mind, the shadows are cowards
It's never easy, follow the need
Make it through alive, plant a new seed
Only one way to go, learning how to grow
Balance the thought, sharing to know

Wrapping things up, only lasts so long
Before the bells, start their ring
Moving inside, shelter from nature
The death of us all, our fate we sing
Rising up again, in our own heads
Feeling the trend, as we go to bed
This is the world, that we have to go through
Anyway you go, ending up blue

**Going Round Again**


Sometimes when I'm digging, a brand new hole
Nothing will stop, cannot control
Feel the roots, from the tree that knows
Could be days or years
Cursed or blessed, call it a quest
What you found, a brand new jest
Rising above, the birds in nest
Letting go my fears

Chorus
Going round again
Another cycle, another trend
Have I been here, will I come again
Nobody knows how the road will end

Other times I rest and looking for signs
Waiting all day, drunk on the wine
Clearing the head, open the mind
Seeing what comes through
Could be the same, repetitive bore
Getting strange, reaching the core
Sun or rain, you can't ignore
The steps in front of you

Chorus

Follow the fool, to find a new trend
Ignoring the rules, the wise man said
Change of the scene, rise from the dead
Walk across the bridge
Into the fog, how far does it go
The troll responded, only you will know
Every step, a past will show
Wide or a razors edge

Chorus

Wake up again, back to the modern world

How far did I fall, the past is a blur
What to do next, become unfurled
Starting over now
A brand new day, what will I do
Dig a hole, or rest for a few
Find a dream, usually end up blue
More fun than a plow

Chorus

**Growing Having Fun**


Run as fast as you can
Climb to the top of the tree
Get to the end
Find the hidden seed

Covered with illusions
A trick with every turn
Plans within plans
All the curtains to unlearn

With water and the sun
Needed in this world
Growing having fun
In the glass that's never full

## Ladders

Building a ladder
One step at a time
Replacing the shatters
The ancients did climb

It used to be a highway
A well traveled road
Then to a flyway
For those in the know

Now a horizon
A star in the night
Stumble when rising
The weight stopping flight

How high can I go
Past repetitive bliss
What will I sew
Nothing to miss


## Lost at Sea

Looking out at new horizons
Feeling stuck on your island
Not content, a state of mind
Seek unknowns, when to climb
Where they end, are found in dreams
Until then, lost at sea

## Quicksands of Time

How can you stand, in quicksands of time
No matter how you move, gone is the land
From under your feet, wishing to fly
Feeling the heat, you cannot deny

Try moving faster, without collateral damage
Ride on the rails, controlling the rampage
Reach for a hand, nobody responds
Ripe for another, message or song

From where it comes, nobody knows
When it arrives, the clocks are broke
Never touching the land or earth
Only thoughts and symbols worth

If received, a ladder is thrown
Yours to climb, for new unknowns
If ignored, a step to remain
Find a group, a stake a claim

But even the steps, of solid foundations
Lose to time in these dimensions
Keeping to climb, higher and lighter
Before the sands, are nothing but fire

## Thirsty Dreams

Feel the rain showering and pouring in your weary head
A wasteland desperately needing a dousing from the dread
From too much racing and skipping on the surface of the dead
Leading towards slipping and falling on a convenient tread
Thoughts of fortune, fame and glory were the stories but instead
Ending up on a scene, broke of dreams, the words no longer said
Let the rain have no restraint to wash away and find the seeds in bed
Help them grow to new unknowns through the infinity in your head


## Trends

Where one dream ends
Another begins
Is the trend
There is no end


## Where the Water Flows

How many times do I need to learn
How many times will I crash and burn
Getting up is much harder than before
When the heights you've gone are feeling to soar
Drop the baggage and what's holding you down
A bit tough at first but after you've found
A more solid place for the wind and rain
With roots to shatter the mirrors that stay
Where it ends, nobody does knows
Riding the boat where the water flows

# Moving On

**End of the Line**

Seeing the signs
But still needing proof
End of the line
Cut free or let loose

**Escaping the Trap**

Wear a disguise, put on a mask
Stay in the new, bury the past
Break all the mirrors, burn up the boat
Cut off the bridge, no bottle or note

Land on a shore, a town from the lore
Keeping head down, marks on the floor
Stopping to rest, catching a jest
Watching the trains, a golden sunset

Buying a ticket, taking a ride
Seeing the lights, passing on by
Look up to the sky, the stars ever still
A question of why, no answer of frills

A thousand stops later, it all seems the same
No longer bother, in hiding your name
Letting it go, all your chips are in
However it falls, start over again

A chance in a million, one at a time
Sooner or later, the odds will align
Dots on a map, lighting a sphere
Escaping the trap, no longer the fear


**Going Someplace New**

One of the things
With going someplace new
So easy to play
The part of a fool

**Goodbye to What is Known**


So many times, when we're all alone
The past comes back, a forgotten throne
The times we fell, like a stone
Into the abyss
What happened next, gotta get away
To the dawn, of a brighter day
Maybe at noon, it'll be ok
The sun burns up the mist

Chorus
It's just the way it goes
Moving on, looking for a home
The rest is gone, the steps are shown
Saying goodbye to what is known

Sometimes you jump, others are pushed
Who can blame, when trending to worse
Like a magnet, drawing in the curse
The signs are everywhere
Stay and fight, dig in your heels
If something more, than surface feels
Or if not, let it go for real
A struggle or a fare

Chorus

Replace it quick, find a new brick
A little different, a brand new trick
Finding fame, pay for kicks
Another tragedy
The joker laughs, has seen it all
Pretty good pun, all the times to fall
Sitting on top of the wall
It's shorter than a flea

Chorus

Try connecting again, to a long lost friend
A different place, or time that blends
The dots are missing, the lines that bend
All the bridges gone
Throw a rope, the gaps too wide
Letting go, what's all outside
Finding the path, we all must climb
This way is much more fun

Chorus

## How Can I Ever Escape

How can I ever escape
From this world that I'm in
Don't even think to tell me it's fate
I'll just throw it in the bin
All I ask is that you can relate
Show me the next plane or train
I'll send you a note from wherever I go
How can I ever escape


## Keeping Calm

Sometimes you try to fit
But it just doesn't work out
Better to up and split
Keeping calm from a shout


## Leaving the Same

Ignoring the rants
Ignoring the raves
Beginning to laugh
Or going insane
From all of the names
That scream from the flame
Having a beer
Leaving the same

## Letting Go

Ignoring the dream
Tragic it seems
Watching it float
Down to the sea
It once was a refuge
A place to escape
Until the reality
Of dragons and snakes
Now I'll let it go
Goodbye and good riddance
Open the windows
Ending the torment


## Moving

It's not so bad
It's not so blue
The only way
To find the new

**Moving Along**


Are you homeless or a real person
Have a job, or should be tried for treason
You're not one of us, clearly stand out
A joker, entertainer, there is no doubt

No, maybe, yes, I'll declare
Not with you, how far do you dare
No harm meant, it 's just a world
No more to expect, hair unfurled

Go back to your drink, call it nature
Dogs at the door, another creature
Do what you will, choices to fill
Repetitive drill, standing still

For me, I'll be moving along
Finding perspectives, write a new song
Never quite finding, where I belong
A child discovering, banging the gong

**No Bother to Stand**


Laws for fear
Abound all around
Feel the tear
For the freedom bound

Starting so simple
Good for the many
Left with a trickle
Slowing the honey

Until the inevitable conclusion
Reaping the end
Minds of illusions
Thinking for rent

Escaping the cage
Anyway you can
Learning to fly
No bother to stand


**Once and for All**


It's just another day in hell
Surrounded by the birds that fell
How can I escape, climb up the wall
Leaving behind, once and for all

**Out of the Glue**

How can I be
Anything new
Unless I escape
Out of the glue


**Phoenix to Awake**

Traveling down the road
Each to our own ends
Always so alone
No sign of a friend

Into the city
Or a far off scene
In another country
The city on the sea

Where the ships sail in
And the music is played
Up all night until
The dawn of the day

Just the way it goes
All plans gone to waste
In the fire we're thrown
The phoenix to wake

## Plans

Plans are like toilet paper
Once put into practice
Should be flushed immediately

## Quitting

Getting up and quitting
Sometimes the right thing to do
When swimming in drivel
Breathing in the new

## Wanderers

We had some good times
There is no doubt
A detour trend
Wanderers throughout

# Hats and Perspectives

## Brain of Boxes

Only so many boxes
Fill up the brain
Some going higher
Others are plain

**Can You**


Can you count the stars
Can you drink to the bottom
Can you rise up again
Can you fill up the platter

Can you fall in love
Can you rise in hate
Can you discard the chains
Can you live to create

Can you hear the screams
Can you see the sorrow
Can you taste the bait
Can you forget tomorrow

Can you walk on water
Can you change your form
Can you get through the tunnel
Can you avoid the norm

I can breathe the air
I can drink my drink
I can feel the moment
I can touch the brink


**From the Mind**


Write a line
From the mind
Pay the price
For the climb


**Hats and Shoes**

All kinds of different hats
Some voluntary or decreed
Blind as a bat
If no shoes on your feet

**Nothing Left to Know**


See the players and their games
Chess or checkers they do play
Moving pieces every day
Which one are you
Maybe a pawn or a king
A queen or knight, bet a ring
In the end, lose everything
Nothing you can do

It started, so long ago
A battle, for your soul
Illusions, no more control
Until nothing, left to know

See the statues watching mirrors
Staying put, being clever
Flowing pride, to the river
It's always the same
One more time, with a stronger sign
More real than real, a sharpened line
Going through, the end of time
Never mind the flames

It started, so long ago
A battle, for a lighter glow
Illusions, no more control
Until nothing, left to know

So confused, which way to go
Passion rules, knowledge flows
Free at last, will to sew
Learning to unlearn
Forgive the lost, the tragedies
Forget the past, trivialities
Find the new, trajectories
Rising from the burn

It started, so long ago
A battle, for a brighter glow

Illusions, no more control
Until nothing, left to know

Step in line and play your part
There for you to wake and start
Call it a dream or star
So much left to do
Yes it's true, it won't be easy
Finding all your, hidden pieces
Where it goes, beyond deceiving
A joke discovered new

It started, so long ago
A battle, for your soul
Illusions, no more control
Until nothing, left to know

**Rising From the Blue**


See the world at war, hear the drums pounding
See the world at peace, hear the flutes sounding
See the world as love, always something new
See the world as hate, call it repetitive dues

Chorus
It's whatever you see, all around you
Making the world, rising from the blue

See the world as old, the sculpture is cast
See the world as a child, new but fast
See the world as big, perspectives galore
See the world as small, chained to the floor

Chorus

See the world as bliss, with a piece of bread
See the world a struggle, alive over dead
See the world as fate, only one way to go
See the world as choice, where the apple grows

Chorus

See the world as easy, finding all the pieces
See the world as hard, a hedge all releasing
See the world as flowing, adapt to the scene
See the world as still, enter the dream

Chorus

**Steps and Bets**

Finding all the steps
Placing all your bets
In the end is shown
Everything you've grown


**The Fool Hat**

So many different hats
Try them all if you can
Laughing without stop
Says the fool when in command


**The Hat**

Of all the different hats
That you might be trying
Only one will be
From which you're relying
It starts in the brain
Growing tall and wide
No matter for rain
With the sun inside

**Walking Through Fire**

Walking through fire
Sought to renew
Evolving much higher
Escaping the blue


**What Is It Worth**

Cursed from birth, what is it worth
Up through the leaves, down for the roots
Define everything, read every book
Reaching the end, no left is took
Call it a cycle, fall from a dream
Aware to adapt, the changing scene


**What to Do**

What is my purpose
What is my thing
Am I to do nothing
Or bells to ring

**Win or Lose**

Sometimes you win
Other you lose
Repetition is down
Up for the new


**Words**

In the day my words
Are all but empty
In the night is strong
With words aplenty